The S
throu

CW00421502

by
Fr Robert Taylerson

All booklets are published thanks to the
generous support of the members of the
Catholic Truth Society

CATHOLIC TRUTH SOCIETY
PUBLISHERS TO THE HOLY SEE

Contents

Introduction

The Scriptures can profitably be read in a variety of ways. They reveal God to us. They may also give us personal help or insight as we reflect on them. Scripture scholars with their skills in exegesis help us to understand the text better. Theologians help us to understand the faith and traditions from scripture which have been handed down.

Key to this book, however, is the confidence that the Scriptures deepen our understanding of prayer. The Scriptures are used here from that more specific but rich perspective. Readers may have a wider or alternative custom of Scripture use. If so I hope that this will be enhanced rather than challenged in the following chapters.

Starting in Genesis, the first book of the Bible, we take a journey through the Old and the New Testaments. No attempt is made to examine every prayer in the Scriptures, rather we look at different forms and images of prayer. Some aspects of faith, understanding of culture and knowledge of significant events are included, as these help our theology of prayer.

Little in this book is my original thought. One source which I have used widely is the *Catechism of the Catholic Church* (*CCC*). Major sources for other insights on prayer and Scriptures are given in the bibliography at the end of this book. I am also grateful to Fr Peter Burrows for a talk given to Birmingham clergy in 2005, for his teaching which helped clarify chapters three and four, to Bishop David McGough, to Fr Paul Dean and to many friends for helpful comments on the text.

Paradise

Imagine paradise. Let your mind range freely. Use whatever images and thoughts come. The first book of the Bible, Genesis, shows a scene before the expulsion of Adam and Eve when God is walking in the garden in the cool of the day. This scene (*Gn* 3:8) is a useful starting point for our reflections.

Imagine yourself in God's company, walking in that garden ... no need for the gift of faith ... no need to believe without seeing. God is here; and takes delight in the beauty of creation. God is at home in that beauty. Nor is God alone. God created us; made us male and female in his own image; more like our Creator than anything else.

We fit into Paradise

In creating humans in his own image and likeness God has given us a nature, which has the ability (and which is intended) to talk to Him, our creator. There is no creature more suited to talking and sharing with Him. When we travel to foreign lands, we often need to wear different clothes, speak different languages, etc. Not so with paradise. We are made to fit in.

The ease with which humans share God's vision

To me the early part of the book of Genesis indicates human ease in God's company. Indeed before the first sin man doesn't argue with God: When God says, "*Be fruitful and multiply. Fill the earth and subdue it. Be masters of the fish in the sea, the birds in the heavens and the beasts of the earth*", Adam doesn't say, "*And how am I supposed to do that?*" He is silent and seems rather to take it for granted that if this is God's will, though he may not understand the way it will unfold, unfold it will.

God said, "It is not right for man to be alone." God wanted individuals not to be solitary, but to live with others as social beings. God wanted a people as well as wanting individuals who are each special.

With the hindsight of Revealed Faith we see that God, "God in the Godhead" is not alone. The Trinity is community. God gives us relationships with others. Our efforts to love them reflect the relationships of the Trinity. God is both creator and community. Adam's essence is in the likeness of God, created an individual, but created to live with and love others.

God wanted Adam to have an ideal helper. God is shown in Genesis making many creatures which didn't fit the bill, until finally woman, flesh from Adam's flesh, bone from Adam's bone, is made. Here again there is no indication that God and Adam had any disagreement about what constituted a suitable mate. It is not as if God said, "Here is a kangaroo for you" and Adam replied, "I'd really prefer a woman." No, there seems to be a unity of views about what is good.

Indeed, man's first words in Scripture are those of a happy response when God made woman (*Gn* 2:23). They express joy at the creation of Eve. We may even see them as the first prayer, when a human being is first shown speaking to God.

Before sin God and mankind seemed in concord. It is post-sin that human conversation with God becomes defensive and more distant. Immediately after the Fall, (in *Gn* 3:9-13), Adam starts guiltily blurting out excuses for sin, to obscure the clarity of the truth. Human sin disrupts that divine/human shared vision which was originally present.

Hope and Paradise

Despite the fact that we are now fallen, walking with God is still a deep call in our hearts. It is wonderful, the ultimate purpose of life, being with Him, sharing in the beauty of God. Looking at His creation, and at God, with thanks and praise, brings us lasting peace. Not only did God pause at the end of the day and see that it was good, but His intention is also that all people delight both in His presence and in His creation.

Many centuries later St Augustine of Hippo was to say to God, *"You have made us for yourself, and our hearts are restless until they find their rest in you."*

One of my favourite understandings about the nature of prayer is that prayer is "the first act of Faith". If we believe then we try to talk with God and we try to listen to God. And so the gift of Faith must inevitably bring about prayer. For fallen humankind it is a life of both frustration and hope: Frustration because I am never going to have that full intimacy with God here; hope because neither do I completely lose it. Yet despite the fact that we are fallen, despite the fact that a mess has been made, both in our nature and through our wills, likeness to God is still present in us. You and I are still made to delight in His presence. This is our ultimate hope, function, and purpose. God has made us so that we can delight in Him and in his presence here on earth. We prepare to delight in His presence forever in heaven.

To such ideas concerning prayer, I would add that contemplation can be understood as "The first act of hope." Through the history of the Christian Church, and also in the history of the Jewish people and other faiths, there is a sense that this "taking time to delight in God's presence" and "committing oneself to intimacy and union with Him" is one of the high callings of prayer. In Christianity the name often now given to this quest and practice is "contemplation".

One of the oft-quoted definitions of contemplative prayer is that of St Teresa of Avila: *"Contemplative prayer in my opinion is nothing else than a close sharing between friends. It means taking time frequently to be alone with Him who we know loves us."*

Concluding reflections

"Delighting in God's presence" is what every human being was made for. It is a form of prayer which is both real now but at the same time leads us to eternal life, where we will be one with God. The same is true of relationships. Our relationships with each other and with God here are real now but also a practice for heaven. The two things take place at the same time. Our present understanding of our loving relationships helps us to understand the beauty of an eternal relationship in and with God.

The Fall

In chapter three of the book of Genesis we see Adam and Eve being thrown out of Eden. They are no longer to share the same physical place with God nor share His vision. By sin humanity turns its back on God. Sin leads to us being banished from God's paradise. It is a tragedy. It is lost intimacy. It brings a rift between God and humankind. There is a rift, too, between humans themselves as they blame others for sin. This is our image from the third chapter of Genesis onwards. The section of the Scriptures which portrays the Fall is not "history" in the sense that a modern historian would define it. Spiritual writers draw truths from it, however, which include some initial understandings of human nature and human behaviour with respect to God and one another.

Let us compare aspects of "Humankind before the Fall" and "Humankind after the Fall".

Before the Fall	After the Fall
Sinless	Sin
Sees God clearly	Sees God in obscurity
Open	Defensive
Free	Restricted
Has nothing to ask for	Has needs

Post-Fall humanity finds things attractive which are neither good nor godly. God seems less present. The shared divine-human vision and concord becomes at best a dimmed, murky vision. Humans become mortal. Death and suffering are experienced. We are unable to live as God intended and the rift cannot be healed by human effort or ability. God's deepest love shown in Christ would be required to atone for that fall from grace.

Learning to ask

Like most people I find it difficult to imagine the Fall. It is an important truth in Jewish and Christian faith, but it is hard to grasp. My difficulty in this is not with the "after" mindset, but rather the "before". In the first chapters of Genesis we see man and woman living a life unaffected by anything which corrupts them. They don't ask God for anything. They are without hurts, without sickness, without hunger, without difficulties in relationships. I find all this hard to imagine. It is beyond my personal experience.

Once the Fall occurs, humans become mortal, suffer, have to labour and live in a world where injustice flourishes. It is a world I recognise. From "not needing to ask" in the first few chapters of Genesis, it is now clear that humans have needs and ought to ask for things. They don't, however, realise this, nor do they know how to ask. Fallen humanity needs to learn. Ideally the person who has sinned would also immediately say, "Sorry", and ask forgiveness. Learning this, however, would be a long process. The human journey towards contrition is lengthy.

Ascending prayer

Part of the "God and Humankind" picture changes as well. Early imagery in the book of Genesis is of man and God together. They are in the same location, able to speak face-to-face. After the expulsion from Eden, however, the more usual image of humanity and God is that God is "up there" and people are "down here" so words addressed to God have to "go up", i.e., ascend.

It is not all so clear-cut, however. There are individuals in the succeeding books of the Hebrew Bible (the Old Testament) who are still portrayed as speaking to God face-to-face. It is wonderful to see individual prophets or patriarchs described in this way. For the rest, with Jewish understanding of the heavens being above the earth, altitude seems sacred. On high mountains of Sinai, Horeb, Zion, etc., they speak their words and send up incense to God "Up there", perceived as a shorter distance from the tops of mountains than from the valleys.

The accepted understanding of pre-Fall prayer is "face-to-face". By contrast, "fallen world" prayer is seen as "ascending", and "hope" can be seen as the route back to "face-to-face".

Seeing God face-to-face

Much could be said about meeting God face-to-face in prayer, e.g., Paul, in the New Testament, writes, "*Now we see dimly ... but then face to face*" (1 Co 13:12). This suggests our current state is one of hope, rather than face-to-face vision. Paul's "*for we walk by faith, not by sight*" (2 Co 5:7) adds the dimension of faith to the spiritual picture. In Christian theology and spirituality the phrase "*beatific vision*" is widely used. This may indicate seeing God face-to-face or may convey a general vision of heaven. I recommend the reader with a particular interest in this topic to pursue this image elsewhere, however (The bibliography gives a useful reference, as I do not attempt to cover its full richness in this book).

Concluding reflections

We started in paradise. The Fall created a gulf between God and us, which we cannot bridge with our own efforts. Yes, the Fall does reduce our clarity of vision of God. We need to ask, to pray to God who seems distant. We are mortal and live with distractions and temptations, which are often strong images in our minds. These may attack even our deepest thirst for prayer. But these attractions have not won. Despite the Fall, easy converse with God is still possible. The differences between the prayer of mortals on this earth and prayer in heaven are real, but need not be huge. God still delights in relationship not only in himself but also with human beings, the pinnacle of his creation. The human ability to pray remains in our nature even in our fallen state, and is encouraged and magnified by God's grace. The journeys of "learning how to say sorry" and "learning how to ask God for what is needed" are long ones, but we must take those journeys.

Covenant

Covenant and prayer

Prayer in the early Jewish tradition includes curses. They are, for me, a difficult part of the tradition. The book of psalms contains three specific cursing (or imprecatory) psalms (*Ps* 57(58), 82(83), 108(109)) and many other psalms have cursing phrases in them. Curses are also found elsewhere in the Hebrew Scriptures.

It was in trying to understand these that I examined the mystery of covenant, and the relationship of covenant with prayer. When I did so, I learned where these prayer-curses were coming from. When I looked at covenant it also led me to the deeper mystery of sacrifice.

Understanding 'covenant'

The Scriptures tell us that God in His love for human beings offered a covenant. But what is a covenant? We live in a world where they are rare. Covenants are generally found in societies where most people don't write. Instead there is a tradition of promises being reliably made and honestly kept. These are an integral part of the community structure, which is vital to that society.

Covenants typically flourished where gods were feared, where communities had very definite identities marked by what they did together, where historical events such as famines and wars created relationships. These events, which cemented people together, were recalled frequently in the community. The early Hebrew Scriptures were written when many tribes and communities fitted these criteria. So we find that the remembering of Hebrew history was integral to the community life. The stories of the history of God's people became their parable. The Jews grew into a community of covenant. They valued sacred vows and promises, and made them with public ritual.

Ritual acts were important to bind the covenant agreement. For example, animals were sacrificed and split in two and the two people who made covenant would walk in between the two halves. The inference of this ritual is to say, "If I break this covenant may I be chopped in two like this animal". Part of the covenant involved calling down the power of God to show that you meant what you said.

Covenant with God involved proclaiming the agreement among the community with God as one's witness. We say that this is what we want and we proclaim it with a solemn oath. The oath brings God into the promise, effectively asking God to bless us if we stand by our words and to curse us if we do not.

God's people invoked Him in covenant and believed in His power. That covenant itself would help to keep them on the straight path. This also shows why for much of salvation history there has been a blurring between words for "prayer" and "sacred vow."

Asking and giving blessings

A further linguistic oddity, which would be taken for granted by speakers of Hebrew, is the language of "blessing" or "blessings". In Hebrew the word for "blessing" is the same as the word for "to respond to a blessing". If God "blesses" us, i.e. gives us favours which bring us joy and gladness, then we, in our turn, "bless" God, i.e. respond in thanks to the "blessings". Both the divine giving and the human response, share the one Hebrew word "*barak*". "Blessing" can mean both the gift from God and our response to that gift.

Concluding reflections

Covenants are solemn agreements, the keeping of which is associated with blessings, the breaking of which with curses. They are vows witnessed to and upheld by the community. Concepts of "blessing", "cursing" and "vows" entered the prayer vocabulary with the first covenants, and have influenced the history of prayer from then on.

Sacrifice

A Note on Livestock

It is almost thirty years since I killed an animal in order to eat it. As a student I kept a few ducks in a poultry shed in the back yard. As the end of term approached and my student grant was running low, one by one I wrung their necks before plucking, drawing and roasting them. Fellow-students eagerly sought invitations to meals. The ducks made a welcome addition to the Sunday lunch plate.

The few hundred animals or part animals which I have eaten since then have been killed by people unknown to me. When I glance over hedgerows, however, I do still see livestock as "units of wealth/business" and as "meals waiting to happen". I can easily understand them also as being potential "units of hospitality" for feasts. Livestock, i.e. animals which were neither pets, nor hunters' prey, were the normal offerings for Hebrew sacrifice. The sense that "what is offered is intended to be consumed", was also taken for granted by the Hebrew people.

In today's society, however, few people have personal experience of agriculture, or of the journey of animals from flock to frying pan. It can be difficult to understand sacrifice if one's first perception of a lamb is as a "cuddly woolly pet" rather than as a "future shared meal" or "something to give to a person whom I esteem". It is also difficult to understand Hebrew sacrifice well if "killing" is too prominent in one's thoughts and "offering" lacks sufficient prominence.

God's first call to sacrifice

Imagine yourself among a people living soon after the Fall. People don't easily recognise God. It is a fallen world. God is not obvious. Imagine God stretching out his hands to us to lead us back to Him. We are becoming His chosen people. We live a real but uneasy and unclear relationship with God. This is the state of people post-Fall in the book of Genesis.

If asked, I would say that I normally communicate with God by listening to His words in the Scriptures and talking to Him in prayer, but that is not how it was then understood. The picture of God's first reaching-out to mankind, the establishment of the first covenant, is found in the ninth chapter of the book of Genesis (*Gn* 9:1-12). Here is the text to put us in the picture. First God gives man dominion over creation, then He says:

"I give you everything. Only you shall not eat flesh with its life, that is to say its blood. For your life-blood I will

surely require a reckoning; of every beast I will require it and of man; . .... Then God said to Noah and to his sons with him, "Behold, I establish my covenant with you and your descendants after you."

(God goes on to proclaim the bow in the heavens, the rainbow, as a sign of this covenant.)

The heart of the initial covenant concerns life-blood, which is God's. The words "life" and "blood" are almost interchangeable. The first communication from God was to do with the sacrifice of animals and their life-blood, which was ritually given to God. Altars were built. Priests were recognised. God was invoked. The covenant was initiated not with a call to pray, but with a call to offer sacrifice.

Blood, sacrifice and offering

God's people sacrificed animals and other forms of life; they were priestly. "Priestly" implies more than "ritual killing". It implies sacrifices offered to God. Blood, by which they understood "life", belonged to God in accord with the covenant they had made. In every living thing there were understood to be two parts, the formal carcass, of which God had given disposition to man, and the blood, the life, which always belonged to God. Every ritual killing of an animal involved pouring blood on or by an altar, or sprinkling blood ritually to show that God was involved, and in each action it was recognised that all life was His. He was the author and master of life, and the first sign and communication of this was by blood.

Within the community of God's people various individuals were called to have a priestly role, acting on behalf of the community, particularly for the blood-offerings and sacrifices. So the start of communication with God was on altars and other places of sacrifice. These also became places of commemoration, where good things were remembered, such as the freedom from floods mentioned by Noah, freedom from slavery, from famine, or the blessing of the harvest.

When God's chosen people through the centuries were unable to offer their daily sacrifice this was often a key time in their growth towards God. They knew there was something wrong. They felt that they weren't living in accordance with how God wanted them to live. The first call from God to Moses which caused Pharaoh's wrath was the call to go into the desert for three days and make sacrifice to God (*Ex* 3:18-20).

Likewise, instructions on offering sacrifice are in prominent positions in the Pentateuch (the first five books of the Hebrew Bible). The first law given to Moses after the ten commandments in the book of Exodus was the law concerning altar and sacrifice (*Ex*

20:22-25). The book of Leviticus starts with the ritual of sacrifice (*Lv* 1:1-27). Chapters four, five and six lead to an understanding that sacrifice can be made for sin.

After the periods of exile, when the people were often unable to keep the sacrificial covenant, we see guilt and sorrow in Jewish community life. First came the covenant, then the ritual practices honouring God as the source and owner of all life. Next came the breaking of that covenant, and only after this came prayers of repentance. No one said "Sorry" for the first human sin, but they did realise there was something wrong when the covenant was not kept.

At times sacrifice was restricted to particular places such as the temple. At other times in Israel's history it was allowed on any wayside altar. With the growth of the temple sacrifice, three-times-a-day sacrifices and offerings came to be associated also with prayers. In addition to the sacrifice of animals, the praying of Scriptures, especially psalms, became a regular habit. Sacrifice was the primary activity, to which prayer became attached. Early indications of this may be found in the first book of Chronicles (1 *Ch* 23:30) where we see the tradition of daily offerings in the temple, and in psalms (*Ps* 55(54):17). The three-times-a-day prayer custom, practiced at the same times as the sacrifices is seen in the book of Daniel (*Dn* 6:10-11). We also find a seven-times-a-day prayer habit, shown in *Ps* 118 (119):164. "*Seven times a day I will praise you.*"

In the temple, sacrifice was always paramount. Prayer was a poor relation. Nor was prayer seen as an obligation in early Hebrew life. Traditions of prayer and the sense of an obligation to pray took time to develop.

Part of the developing tradition of sacrifice was not only the ritual of offering sacrifice, but also the "taking to heart" of the sacrifice. God wanted His people to desire to offer things to their creator with all their hearts.

There is a wonderful example of this in the psalms:

(*Ps* 49/50) "*The God of Gods, the Lord has spoken and summoned the earth. From the rising of the sun to its setting out of Sion's perfect beauty he shines. Our God comes, he keeps silence no longer ... I find no fault with your sacrifices. Your offerings are always before me. I do not ask more bullocks from your farms, nor goats from among your herds ... Do you think I eat the flesh of bulls, or drink the blood of goats? Pay your sacrifice of thanksgiving to God and render him your votive offerings ... A sacrifice of thanksgiving honours me and I will show God's salvation to the upright.*"

The deeper sacrificial offering here is seen in thanksgiving, in keeping God's laws, in being upright, in a contrite heart, the heart that looks to one's neighbour.

The imagery of sacrifices being "consumed" by fire, symbolising them being consumed by God, is also valuable. When I consume food it becomes part of me. When I offer what is mine in sacrifice to God, I want it to be fully accepted. The image of it being "consumed" by God is a good one. Created matter cannot, of course, become part of God. God and created matter would find union only in Jesus, God-made-man. This image of consumption, however, does symbolise full acceptance at a personal level.

Concluding reflections

Starting from a covenant call of God to the people to sacrifice, the Hebrews gradually gain insights into prayer. From the offering of animals and other possessions comes the understanding that greater offerings are contrite hearts, thanksgiving and the offering of oneself to God. From the understanding that life-blood is God's comes a deeper understanding of God in us, of our responsibilities to other people, to other life, and to God's Law.

Learning to Ask

Pagan petitions

Many ways of communication "with gods" were prevalent in the Ancient Near East. For the neighbouring tribes of the Hebrew people, elements of the earth were seen as under the control of different pagan deities (gods), e.g., Baal, the god of thunderstorms, who brought rain and fertility and fecundity to animals.

Pagan prayers always tried to persuade each individual god to do what they wanted because they saw the god as responsible for the blessings or problems with the earth. There were three ways of doing this:

The first was to "butter-up" the god; tell him/her that he/she was wonderful; and ask him/her to deign to do you a favour.

The second way derived from the thought that Baal, or others, really weren't totally free, that gods can have some control exerted over them. This is the false theology which today we would associate with incantations ... the idea that if prayers are said in a particular way, and if they are accompanied by a particular ritual, then the god would have no option but to do what he was told.

The third way, for many primitive tribes, was to see prayer in terms of a proposed "deal" with the god. Man promises the god a service and asks for a service in return.

Throughout human history there has always been a gut reaction in humanity to want gods to be controllable or vulnerable to flattery, to want prayers that are guaranteed to work, that leave god(s) without the freedom to say "No", or to see prayer as a "business transaction", or "deal".

Incantation terminology

The terminology of speaking to gods in the Ancient Near East always sought to develop powerful words and rites of prayer. Some Akkadian prayers, those of neighbouring tribes of the Hebrew people, had formulae where every line of the prayer would start with a different letter of the alphabet until each letter was used. This gave an idea of "perfect" prayer, and there was a feeling that, if these prayers were used with correct rituals, the gods would be obliged to accede to the petitions. With some traditions the need for the prayer to be perfect was so esteemed that every mistake or halt was seen to make a prayer valueless. In the history of Jewish prayers, similar alphabetic structures can be found, as can phrases from the prayers of other religions. Their culture is not free from such influence. The wise leaders of the Jewish people, however, always tried to assure those who kept the Lord as their true God that he was protector, creator, and leader, but he was also free, i.e., He could say "No".

There is some evidence, too, that early Jewish prayers did not have an obligatory formula of words beyond opening and closing phrases, although they did have a fixed structure. In this respect they differed from many neighbouring tribes, for whom each and every word of prayer was fixed. Today, contemporary Jewish prayers have a more fixed pattern of words, though the awareness of God's freedom to say "No" is still present.

Not asking

Perhaps what seems most odd to our Christian eyes is the scarcity of prayers in the early books of the Bible that are simply prayers of petition. For instance, when Hagar and Ishmael face starvation (*Gn* 21:15-21) they don't turn to God and say "Please give us something to eat." Rather God hears sobbing ... and acts with compassion. Humans haven't learned to pray. They haven't learned to turn to God when in need.

In a similar way, Abraham fails to plead for his son Isaac's life in Genesis chapter twenty-two. When

Sodom and Gomorrah are threatened with destruction (*Gn* 18), Abraham engages in a prayer something like oriental haggling, and although the process runs its course, the goal is not reached. Generally, when we see man asking for something in the earlier books of the Old Testament it is only after God has taken an initiative. The habitual or spontaneous asking of things from God comes later.

Jewish petition theology

In Jewish daily prayer books today there is a more limited theology of the power of intercessory prayer than in the Christian tradition. Perhaps this is because of a good desire to keep far away from anything resembling incantations. The introduction to the current Jewish Morning and Evening Prayer Book suggests that the traditional Jewish understanding of prayer has three characteristics:

1. *"The text is fixed, as are the times for prayer.*
2. *The composition of texts includes teachings as well as petitions.*
3. *The liturgy, usually worded in the plural form, is intended for community rather than private recitation.*

"...These characteristics provide the answer to what seems to Jewish theology to be the obvious problems of prayer:

1. *Does the all-knowing God require the articulation of our needs when he knows them already?*
2. *How can we hope to change his will? Our belief in the efficacy of our prayer seems to challenge his immutability, perhaps even his justice, since we should assume that whatever fate he decrees for us is just. Why seek to reverse it?"*

Such Jewish theology sees prayer as more concerned with being formed by God than with changing things outside the community. The prayer-book introduction continues:

"Like sacrifice, prayer is meant to bring mankind near to God. The understanding is that we need prayer to bring us close to God.

The Hebrew word for prayer, tephillah comes from hithpallel, meaning to judge oneself. Jewish theology sees prayer more as imprinting God and His will on the community than as effecting a change outside the community. The harder I pray the more convinced I become that only God can help me, and the more I need his help. Prayer thereby turns me into a better and more deserving human being in respect to the favours for which I ask."

Concluding reflections

Human instincts rarely change. There may be present in our minds, consciously or unconsciously, a tendency to 'butter-up', 'do a deal with God', or 'find a perfect set of words which God has no power to avoid agreeing to'.

A prominent Jewish understanding of the purpose of asking God in prayer, is that the minds of the individuals and of the community become more attuned to God's will and more accepting of it.

There are some wonderful truths in the above outline of Jewish theology of prayer. The understanding of prayer as something used by God to form the individual or the community is an important image, probably underused today in Christian circles.

The Jewish theology of intercession described above is, however, from a Christian perspective, ultimately incomplete. The New Testament makes it clear that part of the function of prayer is to "badger" God for what seems to us to be good. When what is good or right is absent, we are to keep on asking in the hope and expectation that this prayer will be efficacious.

Abraham and Jacob

Abram/Abraham: man of trust

Abraham, a great father of the Hebrew people, is not a man who has given us either models of prayer or particular phrases of prayer. He was, however, recognised as a man of great trust in God, and of faith, essential virtues in all who pray. (*CCC* 2570-2572)

Abraham persevered in his discussions with God, despite the fact that things didn't always work out as he expected. When Abram had been promised children but hadn't received them, he turned to God and said, *"'O Lord God, what wilt thou give me for I continue childless and the heir of my house is Eliezar of Damascus?', and Abram said, 'Behold thou hast given me no offspring, and the slave born in my house will be my heir'. And behold, the word of the Lord came to him and said, 'This man shall not be your heir, your own son shall be your heir.' And he brought him outside and said, 'look toward heaven and number the stars if you are able to number them.' Then he said to him, 'So shall your descendants be'. And he believed the Lord...".* (*Gn* 15)

That sense of trust continued through Abram/ Abraham's life. We see Abraham also as being the first person to "have a go" at intercession for Sodom and Gomorrah (*Gn* 18) He is not held up as a paragon of intercessory prayer ... it didn't go far enough, but he is the first person to try.

Abraham has a good "Prayer Personality"

In his desire to intercede for others and attain God's mercy for them, Abraham can be favourably contrasted with the later prophet Jonah. Abraham was keen that the people of Sodom and Gomorrah be spared the wrath of God, and immediately set about haggling with God to this end. Jonah, the reluctant prophet on the other hand, is depicted as not interceding for the people of Nineveh, and as being unhappy when they repented and received God's mercy (*Jon* 4:1-11).

The comparison shows not only of a difference in character, but also in enthusiasm for prayer. In scriptural accounts of a person's eagerness to pray we may find criteria with which we can assess our own prayer lives. We are helped to reflect on our own "prayer personality".

Another of Abraham's virtues is the willingness to offer more than animal sacrifice, something of himself. He offered his own son as a sacrifice at what he perceived to be God's behest. It was not ultimately called upon, thanks to God's intervention, but the willingness to offer his son, something of himself in sacrifice, takes our understanding of "sacrifice" beyond animal offerings to the "giving of self."

Jacob: wrestling in prayer

The first person in Genesis to whom a model of prayer has been attributed was Jacob. The key event in terms of prayer is his all-night wrestling bout found in *Gn* 32. Jacob sends his family across the ford, and then he has a wrestling match:

"And a man wrestled with him until the breaking of the day. When the man saw that he did not prevail against Jacob he touched the hollow of his thigh, and Jacob's thigh was put out of joint as he wrestled with him. Then he said, 'Let me go for the day is breaking', but Jacob said, 'I will not let you go unless you bless me'. And he said to him, 'What is your name?', And he said, 'Jacob'. Then he said, 'Your name shall no more be called Jacob, but Israel', for you have striven with God and with men, and have prevailed'. Then Jacob asked him, 'Tell me, I pray, your name.' But he said, 'Why is it that you ask my name?' And there he blessed him, so Jacob called the name of the place Peniel, saying, 'For I have seen God face to face and yet my life is preserved'."

This is a very odd passage. This sense of prayer being a battle or tussle or wrestling match has been gained from it and used in writings on prayer again and again. It is often cited to encourage us to 'keep on going for it!' in our own prayer.

Jacob is physically harmed by his thigh being put out of joint, while at the same time he is blessed by his opponent. Jacob is both wounded and blessed by God in his wrestling. Following this incident he seeks out his brother Esau and becomes reconciled with him.

Wounded and Blessed

The sense of being wounded as well as blessed through intense prayer continues in the Judaeo-Christian tradition. The best-known example in later Christian writings may be found in the first stanza of John of the Cross's "*Spiritual Canticle*", "*You fled like the stag after wounding me*". "God's love for the beloved" and "the harming of God's beloved" may both be real and happening at the same time. The image of prayer leading to being harmed is unpalatable. I can understand that being harmed does lead to greater dependence on God and others. It does make it more obvious that any power comes **through** the harmed person rather than **from** them. But at the same time it begs the question Is harm necessary? and if so, why? This question leads ultimately to the mystery of the suffering of Jesus. Only in this mystery can harm or brokenness be understood.

In addition to the wrestling, we have Jacob's phrase, "I have seen God face-to-face." Having fallen from paradise mankind no longer expects to see God face-to-face. It is a special privilege when he does.

God-walkers

Early in the book of Genesis two characters, Enosh (or Enoch), and Noah, are each described as "walking with God" (*Gn* 5:24, 6:9 [*CCC* 2569]). As with the phrase face-to-face, these accounts bring to mind images of unfallen humankind in Eden. The accounts of their lives indicate that they were more upright and God-fearing than their contemporaries. The "walking with God" and the blessing of long lives are seen as signs of God's favour, leading to more intimacy with God.

Concluding reflections

We are helped to learn to pray, in part, by pondering individuals' personal stories such as those above. Trust, woundedness, being blessed, one's prayer-personality and other aspects may all play a part.

Moses

The events of Moses' life and his role as an intermediary between God and the people shed further light on prayer. A good place to start is at the burning bush:

Reverence (*Ex* 3:1-10)

"Now Moses was keeping the flock of his father-in-law, Jethro, the priest of Midian, and he led his flock to the west side of the wilderness and came to Horeb, the mountain of God. And the angel of the Lord appeared to him in the flame and fire out of the midst of a bush. And he looked and lo the bush was burning; yet it was not consumed. And Moses said, "I will turn aside and see this great sight; why the bush is not burnt". When the Lord saw that he turned aside to see, God called to him out of the bush "Moses, Moses!" He said, "Here am I." And he said, "Do not come near. Put off your shoes from your feet. For the place on which you stand is holy ground." And he said, "I am the God of your father, the God of Abraham, the God of Isaac, and the God of Jacob." And Moses hid his face for he was afraid to look at God. Then the Lord said, "I have seen the affliction of

my people who are in Egypt, and have heard their cry because of their taskmasters. I know their sufferings and I have come down to deliver them out of the hand of the Egyptians and to bring them up to that land, to a good and broad land, a land flowing with milk and honey ..."

Various things are happening. First the events take place on a mountain, seen in Hebrew thought as being "nearer to heaven". Second, we see God's presence coming down on the earth. We see a rare manifestation of God not in heaven but on earth, in the burning bush. Third, we see Moses being told to have reverence, and take off his shoes. This may be seen as the first example of a personal act of reverence in the Scriptures (though prostration (*Gn* 18:2) may also be cited). We then see the call of Moses. We see Moses being afraid, hiding his face before God. Moses is not comfortable. He is timid.

Growing in intimacy

When Moses entered the tent of meeting in the desert, the pillar of cloud would descend and the Lord would speak with Moses. When all the people saw the pillar of cloud at the entrance to the tent, they would all rise up and worship, every man at his tent-door. *"Thus the Lord used to speak to Moses face to face as a man speaks to his friend."* (*Ex* 33:11) ... What a lovely witness in our fallen world! Union with God is not completely broken. God still occasionally visits those he has chosen in a special way.

In the same chapter of Exodus (*Ex* 33:18-20) God refuses to let Moses see him in glory, saying that man cannot see his face and live. When Pope Benedict reflects on this passage in his book, "Jesus of Nazareth", his understanding is that mankind will see God to the fullest only in Jesus.

Moses' humility

Moses is not portrayed as a man whose natural qualities make him powerful. He has a speech impediment and he lacks confidence in himself. He gets Aaron to help him. Numbers 12:3 describes Moses as *"A humble [or meek] man, the most humble man on earth"*. Yet he is the one who is speaking to God as a friend. Moses then finds out things about God. God shares with him:

"The Lord passed before him and proclaimed, "The Lord, The Lord, a God merciful and gracious; slow to anger and abounding in steadfast love and faithfulness; keeping steadfast love for thousands, forgiving iniquity and transgression and sin ..." (*Ex* 34:5-7)

This is a prelude to the giving of the ten commandments. Amidst the strict justice and law we find a God who is, *"Slow to anger and rich in steadfast love and faithfulness."* The power of God is shown with an image of mercy, steadfast love. These qualities of a loving

God are shared with Moses. An understanding of God's love is a gift, which often comes through humble prayer.

Confidence – Moses becoming an intermediary between God and his people

Moses is the best Old Testament example of an intermediary between God and the people (*CCC* 2574-2576). He intercedes for the people. Our word "intercede" implies a "go-between". A good example is the battle between the Israelites and the Amalekites. (*Ex* 17:9-13):

"Moses said to Joshua, "Choose for us men and go out, fight with Amalek tomorrow and I will stand at the top of the hill with the rod of God in my hand". ...Whenever Moses held up his hand, Israel prevailed; and whenever he lowered his hand Amalek prevailed. But Moses' hands grew weary, so they took a stone and put it under him and he sat upon it, and Aaron and Hur held up his hands, one on one side and the other on the other side, so that his hands were steady until the going down of the sun. And Joshua mowed down Amalek and his people with the edge of the sword."

Moses intercedes for the people, putting himself between them and God, hands upright. The first paintings we see of Christians in the catacombs show the same "orantes" position, the position of prayer with hands raised in the same way. The tradition continues.

When I hold up my hands in prayer liturgically, it has the same indication of prayer of intercession, of petition, of asking God for good things.

Intercession for sinners

Moses has confidence to stand up before God even for people who have done wrong and deserve punishment. He pleads when Pharaoh asks him to plead with God to end the plagues. Moses does so, but then the heart of Pharaoh changes. Similarly he pleads for Miriam, who becomes leprous. Aaron says to Moses, *"O my Lord do not punish us because we have been foolish and sinned. Let her not be as one of the dead...."* (*Nb* 12:11 ff) Aaron recognises that Miriam and he have done wrong. Moses pleads with God. After seven days' quarantine, Miriam is brought back, healed, in response to Moses' prayer.

The above examples are models of prayer and intercession which Moses has given to the tradition, and which we reflect on, learn from, and still treasure in the Church today.

Concluding reflections

Moses gives us a good example of reverence, confidence, humility and courage, in his intercession and intimacy with God.

Psalms

What are the Psalms?

The earliest Hebrew texts do not give this book a name. Our word "Psalm" comes from the Greek word *Psallo*, which means "to sing accompanied by a plucked string instrument". The nearest Hebrew equivalent is the word *Mizmor*, though it is little used. The more common Hebrew word for psalms is *Tehillim*, meaning "Hymn". Some groups of psalms are also referred to as *Tephilloth*, meaning "prayers".

Who wrote them?

Some scholars see the book of psalms as the hymn book of the second temple in Jerusalem (built approx. 500 B.C.) A large number directly claim to be written by David himself. (All the psalms are attributed to King David, but much of this is honorific).

How are they numbered?

The psalms, as we have them now, number one hundred and fifty. The Hebrew Bible was translated into the Greek (the Septuagint) before 400 BC. In the process some psalms were split in half and others were joined together, so the numbering of the Greek psalms has always been different from the Hebrew. For most psalms it is one less than the Hebrew number, e.g. *"The Lord is my Shepherd"* begins the psalm numbered twenty-three in Hebrew and twenty-two in Greek.

What is contained in the Psalms?

Jewish teachers tried to encourage people to see in the psalms all that was most rich in the Hebrew Bible. The psalms were traditionally split into five books, to mirror the Pentateuch, the five most important books of the Jewish Scriptures.

The more common way to group the psalms, however, is according to their form or use in the Jewish liturgy. So they are grouped according to whether they are psalms of praise, of individual lament, of group lament, of thanksgiving, processional psalms, penitential psalms, royal psalms etc.

Are there key Psalms?

Jewish understanding

In Jewish tradition, Psalms 1 and 2 are seen as the prelude to the Psalter. They also explain what it is all about. *"Happy indeed is the man who follows not the way of the wicked ...*" etc. Human beings conforming to God, is the key. The perspective with which to start looking at the psalms is that of the covenant. The sense is "Do good and be blessed, or do bad and be cursed; look to see what you are doing!"

A further insight comes with Psalm 1:2, which declares happy/blessed the person who ponders/meditates the Law.

A note on "Meditation" of Psalms

The early Jewish practice of the process of meditation involved saying or singing the words of Scripture over and over again with the understanding that they then "sink in" and begin to guide one's life. Meditation is thus the equivalent of mumbling/ruminating/chewing the cud. Meditation on the Law (the Pentateuch) was encouraged, and the psalms were texts to be repeated day and night in order to shape one's life. Later Christian usage expanded the concept of "meditation", but we still also "meditate" according to the original use of the word. Seeing psalms as texts for meditation is central to the Jewish understanding of their use and purpose.

We might question whether Psalm 1 is actually a prayer at all, because it seems neither to speak to God, nor to ask, nor to thank, nor to involve any of the actions which we commonly define as prayer. Prayer is commonly concerned with words **to** God, whereas hymns are more commonly words **about** God. Saint Augustine later defines hymns in terms of song, and the praise of God, "*It is a song with praise of God.*" Many psalms are more hymn-like than prayer-like.

In the Christian era we have downplayed the Hebrew understanding of some prayers as being "texts used to impress the knowledge of God and his will on individuals and communities" (cf. Chapter 5). This has impoverished our vision of prayer. Just as every advertising executive knows, putting images and texts in our minds repeatedly does influence our perspectives, our choices and our actions. Singing and meditation of the psalms helps God's imprint to be pressed more deeply and clearly on our lives.

Christian understanding

In the Christian tradition the invocation "*O God come to our aid.*" and its response "*O Lord make haste to help us*" (*Ps* 69/70:1) are well known. This is thanks to John Cassian, a fourth century monk who brought the Egyptian monastic wisdom to the West. In his tenth conference he taught this phrase as the key to all the psalms. Cassian saw it as conveying all feelings, as a shield against all temptation, as expressing the humility of pious confession, our frailty, our confidence in being heard etc. The core of the psalms in his viewpoint is our crying out to God because He is our help, our shield, our protector, and our guide.

A Note on "Asking" in the Psalms

The early Christian Church was very focussed on prayer as petition, which undoubtedly affected the way psalms were read. A large number of psalms are psalms of lament, which cry "Help!" for individuals and communities in many different circumstances. Several psalms are also very penitential in character, asking forgiveness in mature and beautiful ways.

So, although "asking God's aid and help" may seem to be rather limited as a "key understanding of the psalms", it does have something to be said for it. Asking in prayer was perhaps deficient in earlier Hebrew Scriptures, but it is certainly not deficient in the psalms.

What purposes do the different Psalms have?

Praise

Many psalms are psalms of praise e.g. the last five (146-150), as well as others found elsewhere in the Psalter. The word "Alleluia" is frequently used. It simply means "Praise the Lord God". Alleluia is a Hebrew word. The etymology may be as follows: *Hallelu* = Praise, and *Yah* (from "Yahweh") = the Lord God.

Liturgy

We can identify some psalms as having a specific place in worship. "*Burnt offering I bring to your house, the vows my lips have uttered*" (*Ps* 65/66:13), is associated with daily offerings in the temple. "*Go round Sion; walk right through her ...*" (*Ps* 47/48:12-13), talks of walking (processing) to and through Sion, i.e., Jerusalem. Some psalms describe liturgy in more detail. "*Open for me the gates of saving justice ... this is the gate of the Lord where the just may enter*" (*Ps* 117/118:19-20) refers to the temple gates, through which people go to make offerings. "*I wash my hand in innocence and join the procession around your altar, O Lord*" (*Ps* 25/26:6), talks of ritual washing associated with the temple sacrifices.

Ascent

A set of psalms, (119/120 to 131/132) are called "psalms of Ascent". They are thought to have been composed for, and used by, pilgrims to Jerusalem.

Others

Some psalms of praise are traditionally sung by the Jewish people in their daily prayer, e.g. Psalm 144/145, which blesses God, "*I will extol you, O God, my king, I will bless your name forever ...*". Other psalms used in daily prayer give thanks for God's blessings, e.g., Psalm 29/30, "*I will extol you, O Lord, you have lifted me up and have not let my enemies rejoice over me"*. This expresses confidence and trust, appropriate for daily life, as does Psalm 90/91, *"He who dwells in the shelter of the most high, and abides in the shade of the almighty says to the Lord 'My refuge, my stronghold, my God in whom I trust'"*.

In addition to those psalms which are routinely used in worship in praise and thanksgiving, there are also other genres. Some are penitential, remembering and renewing sorrow. From Psalm 103/104 onwards we find a selection of psalms which savour God's marvels and his presence in Hebrew history. The people's history was their parable, and it is nowhere better expressed than in psalmody.

Concluding reflections

In the psalms we find hymns for almost every emotion and occasion of human life. They help us to live our lives in God's presence whatever happens. They provide for both community prayer and individual prayer. The keeping of God's Law is promoted. There are personal cries for help when in need. As a collection, the psalms encourage meditation, praise, repentance, lament, thanksgiving, reflection on one's history, and worship. Above all, however, the psalms are a river in which to immerse ourselves, so that they become the spiritual environment of each person's heart.

Samuel, David and Solomon

Samuel, learning from "God and Eli"

Early in the book of Samuel we encounter the prayer of Hannah, Samuel's mother, (1 S 2:1-10) and her generous giving of her son into the temple service. Samuel soon hears a voice he doesn't recognise. The priest Eli realises that Samuel is hearing God's voice. Eli tells Samuel that if he hears the voice call again he should say, "*Speak, Lord, your servant is listening.*" What a basic instruction! When God speaks to you, recognise that it might be him and say to him, "Yes, I want to listen." It's the first bit of teaching in prayer that we see in the Scriptures. A man of prayer starts to instruct an apprentice in prayer. It is a wonderful example, and so simple. Many of us are taught **both** directly by God **and** by those experienced in prayer.

Obligation

The growing understanding that Samuel is called to prayer eventually makes him recognise that prayer is not only part of his vocation, but is also an obligation. For example, after Saul had been chosen as king and the people asked Samuel to pray for them, he says: *"Moreover, as for me, far be it from me that I should sin against the Lord by ceasing to pray for you, and I will instruct you in the good and the right way"*. (1 S 12:23)

What awareness! Samuel has recognised that it would be sinful if he, Samuel, stopped praying for God's people. This is the start of the understanding that there is an obligation to pray. In the Pentateuch the obligation to offer sacrifice is clear, as is the obligation to keep God's laws and commandments. The sense of there being an obligation to pray, however, is not prominent. Prayer-obligation is a later development in Judaism. This text is a very early example of the recognition of this obligation.

David's dancing: reverence and joy

The episode when David dances before the Ark of the Covenant (2 S 6) witnesses to the Lord's presence making a place holy. It is David's pride and joy to have the Ark with him so he leaps up and down in God's honour. Just as we saw Moses' reverence at the burning bush, so we see David's reverence, in a different form, by the Ark.

Solomon: asking for the best of gifts

Solomon's request for wisdom (1 K 3) is prayer that asks for the best of God's gifts. At Gideon the Lord appeared to Solomon in a dream by night. God asked what he should give him. Solomon asked not for riches but for understanding and wisdom. God was pleased with this and gave it to him. Asking for wisdom was taken as a model request for kings and leaders of Israel. Wisdom given by God became highly esteemed.

Concluding reflections

God teaches me to pray. God may enlist others to teach me also. Having reverence is part of praying well. We are commended to pray for wisdom, and other gifts with which we help to build God's kingdom. Prayer is also an obligation.

Suffering and Prayer: Job and Isaiah

Job: the just and suffering, interceding for sinners

Many scriptural images indicate that the just may intercede for sinners. Moses intercedes for Aaron, who made the golden calf, for Miriam, for Pharaoh, and others. Sometimes intercession is more powerful in a person who has had a particularly testing experience. The story of Job is a good example: Job was the archetypical "man who never did anything wrong" yet bad things happened to him one after another. The men whom we call "Job's comforters" interpret Job's early disasters, thinking that God always blesses those who do good in their life on earth and God always curses those who do evil. Their reasoning is "Bad things happen to you, Job; therefore you must be doing something wrong! You must deserve it!" As the book of Job progresses, we are led to a deeper understanding of blessings and curses.

Older Jewish Theology

Jewish history was steeped in an earlier tradition of "life without personal resurrection." Blessings were seen simply in terms of this earthly life.

Newer Theology

By the time the book of Job was written, Jewish theology was starting to glimpse the hope of personal resurrection. Blessings are then no longer simply interpreted as "in this life." God's people grow in the hope of the promise of what is to come.

Job's power of prayer

After all the bad things happen, God turns Job's life around, and Job is blessed in this life. After the Lord has spoken to Job, The Lord speaks to one of "Job's comforters", Eliphaz the Temonite and says,

"My wrath is kindled against you and against your two friends; for you have not spoken of me what is right, as my servant Job has. Now therefore take seven bulls and seven rams and go to my servant Job and offer up for yourselves a burnt offering, and my servant Job shall pray for you. For I will accept his prayer not to deal with you according to your folly. For you have not spoken of me what is right as my servant Job has. So Eliphaz the Temonite and Bildad the Shuhite and Zuphar the

Naamathite went and did what the Lord had told them;
and the Lord accepted Job's prayer." (Jb 42)

This is a gem of a text! We realise that the power of
Job as an intercessor has grown through his faithfulness
in all the trials and difficulties which beset him. He is
shown as someone who has more prayer-power than
others. As God blesses Job, his "comforters" recognise
that they have been wrong. They need Job's prayer.
Their own prayer lacks the power of Job's.

Isaiah's suffering servant

There is a yet more profound witness to the power of
individuals' intercession, Isaiah's fourth "song of the
suffering servant". "*Yet it was the will of the Lord to
bruise him; he has put him to grief; when he makes
himself an offering for sin he shall see his offspring, he
shall prolong his days; the will of the Lord shall prosper
in his hand; he shall see the fruit of the travail of his soul
and be satisfied. By his knowledge shall the righteous one,
my servant, make many to be accounted as righteous.*"

In this passage, (*Is* 53), the self-offering of one who
suffers is seen as powerful atonement for sin. It mirrors
Job's power of prayer after his trials but carries with it a
deeper understanding of "offering".

These examples show the nature of a "type" of a
prayerful person who aspires to communion with God
and who perseveres in steadfastness, generosity and

hope even through trials. They deepen the earlier association of prayer, sacrifice and offering.

Concluding reflections

These examples remind us of the need not to see our prayer lives in isolation, but to understand them as integral to our wider lives of faith, our trials and difficulties, and our striving for virtue. My personal trials, if I am faithful, may enable me to intercede better for others.

The Gospel Canticles

In the Hebrew Bible the greatest hymns are the psalms. Among the New Testament hymns the four Gospel canticles take pride of place. They are found at the start of Luke's Gospel. They act as hinges of prayer between the Old and New Covenant, and are prophetic of Christ, but also give thanks for the fulfilling of God's promises. The shortest is the song of the angels ...(*Lk 2:14*) *"Glory to God in the highest and on earth peace to men on whom his favour rests."* (We have transformed this into the start of the *Gloria* at Mass). The three others are as follows:

The *Magnificat* (*Lk 1:46-55*) is the canticle of Mary, who is visiting Elizabeth, both happy in their pregnancies. Mary rejoices in the blessings to come. Like most scriptural hymns it is about God, but not addressed directly to God. Many of its phrases echo the song of Hannah in the first chapter of the book of Samuel. Mary proclaims her joy in the coming of her Son with humility and with thanks to God. The *Magnificat* teaches us how to praise and give true thanks whilst living in humility. It starts from the perspective of the personal. *"My soul glorifies ..."* and then gives thanks for wider blessings to the community, "*He has come to the help of* **Israel** ..."

Mary gives us many models for prayer. It was she who generously said "*Let it be done according to your word*", who pondered holy events in her heart, who asked her Son to help others deepen their joy in celebration (at Cana), who was present when her son suffered, showing deep compassion. In all this she is a powerful witness and ally in our prayer. In the prayer of the *Magnificat* she gives us an unsurpassed model in prayer of humility, thanks and service to God.

The *Benedictus* (*Lk* 1:68-79) is the canticle of Zechariah. He had been struck dumb for some time; then he was called upon to proclaim his son's name, "John". He foresaw, and welcomed, a future in God's service for his son and joyfully proclaimed this canticle. Like the *Magnificat* it is about God but not addressed to God. It refers to John and the Saviour (Christ) whom John was to proclaim as the fulfilment of the Old Testament prophecies.

The previous dumbness of Zechariah is an important prelude to this prayer. We are glad to join him in the knowledge that, whatever else is lacking, God today gives us a voice with which to bless Him, and to proclaim our belief in the fulfilment of His promises in Christ. The *Benedictus* is for us a wonderful model prayer of witness and hope.

The third canticle, the *Nunc Dimittis* (*Lk* 2: 29-32), comes from the lips of Simeon, the elderly man in the temple, who had served God with his life, and who had received a revelation that he would not die until he had set eyes on the Saviour. Unlike the *Magnificat* and *Benedictus*, Simeon does talk directly to God. Simeon proclaims to God, his master, that his life is joyfully fulfilled at the sight of the Saviour, Jesus, whom Mary and Joseph had come to present in the temple.

As I pray the Gospel canticles I often bring to mind a picture of Mary, Zechariah and Simeon who Luke portrays first proclaiming them. When I pray the *Nunc Dimittis* I imagine Simeon as an elderly man, but nevertheless dancing with joy as he proclaims his happiness to be in the presence of the Saviour. It reminds me of the happiness I should have with Christ in our midst, and renews in me the comfort of Christ's presence.

Concluding reflections

In the Gospel canticles, the *Magnificat*, *Benedictus* and *Nunc Dimittis*, we find songs that we, the Christian assembly, have taken as our own. They are special texts which help us to follow Christ, to praise God and to express the thanksgiving which is appropriate not only to Mary, to Zechariah and Simeon, but to each and every Christian. They are model texts for prayer.

Jesus' Teaching and the Our Father

Some Christians writing about prayer centuries after the Resurrection would rightly include a consideration of the divine nature of Jesus. In so doing they would see Jesus both as "Son", and as one to whom we pray, as God. In the Gospels, however, we do not see anyone praying to Jesus as God, nor do we see Jesus encouraging others to address him in prayer. Jesus is a person who prays, and who teaches his friends to pray.

Before looking at the "Our Father", let us consider four preliminaries.

First: the use of words

Jesus teaches those who follow him not to put a greater value on words than they deserve. Prayer does not consist in the repetition of the words *as the gentiles do (Mt 6:7)*, i.e., words have no magic value which will guarantee success. Mere wordiness doesn't equal more prayer.

Also we must not pray *like the hypocrites who look for the best places in the synagogues and want to be seen (Mt 6:5)*. We must pray in secret to the Father who sees us in secret. And we must persevere in prayer. (We shall look more at perseverance when we consider the parables.)

Second: necessary attitudes

Jesus makes it quite clear that there are conditions to fulfil in order that prayer be heard.

1. Asking for material things is fine, but it is always better to search for the kingdom of God and its justice. The rest will be given to you as an extra (*Mt* 6).

2. In the same way, when asking for pardon for sins we must be willing to forgive others their wrongs. (*Mt* 6:12, 6:14, 18:21 18:35. *Mk* 11:25 11:26. *Lk* 11:4, 17:4).

3. It is not enough to say, "*Lord, Lord*," to enter the kingdom of heaven. In fact, any such prayer would be false if one is not willing to carry out the will of the Father (see *Mt* 7:21-23 and parables which stress acting correctly, such as the good Samaritan.)

In addition to the above he tells us that we can join together in asking in his name. In a community of prayer Jesus is in our midst. He is a mediator of prayer and of forgiveness. This gives a perspective that is not found in the Jewish tradition.

When we look at Jesus' overall teaching, he doesn't give specific instructions on prayer or adoration, or worship, or praise, or blessing or acts of thanks, which

Judaism already practised. He does show them in his life. He also invites us to pray with penitence, turning our hearts to God with faith in the good news.

Third: the need for faith

Trust in God is taught by Jesus as an essential for petitionary prayer. The synoptic Gospels (those of Matthew, Mark and Luke) give us several extreme examples. The most vivid is the image of faith as tiny as a mustard seed being enough to move mountains (*Mt* 17:20. *Lk* 17:6). Trustfulness is shown at its most extreme when Jesus indicates that when we ask in prayer, we should believe we have already obtained it, and it will be ours. (*Mk* 11:23-24, *Mt* 21:21-22).

Fourth: scriptural "prayer" words in the new testament

What does "pray" mean in English outside a religious context? (e.g. in the phrase ... "Pray, tell me") ... The answer is simply "to ask politely" or to "petition". Today we are used to a broad range of meanings for the word "pray". We have, in religious texts, stretched its use.

The exact meaning of words at any particular time is not easy to pinpoint. Most of the Greek prayer-words (*euche, proseuchomai, deesis etc.*), however, posess a sense of requesting. For the majority of the words that we see translated into English in the New Testament as "pray", the Greek is much more likely to indicate making a request than is our current English expanded use of the word "pray". It is a mistake to expect something broader than the language (Greek) then allowed. And so when Matthew's and Luke's Gospels show Jesus telling his friends "pray like this" and giving them the Our Father, the Greek word used is *"proseuchomai"* which has the same sense as English, "asking". The friends of Jesus are, in effect saying, "Teach us how to request things from God".

There are two versions of the Our Father. Matthew gives us the prayer taught to the disciples within a general context of teaching about prayer. It is found in the Sermon on the Mount. Luke, by contrast, explains that the disciples *asked Jesus how to pray, "... just as John the Baptist taught his own followers."* John's followers would have known and kept the usual Jewish pious practices in synagogues, home and temple. This prayer they requested was something more.

The "Our Father" texts (*Mt* 6: 9-13, *Lk* 11:2-4)

There are some differences between the two versions of the "Our Father". Luke's text opens with an invocation identical to that used elsewhere by Jesus ... *"Father"* (in Aramaic *"Abba"*) as in Mark's Gospel (*Mk* 14:36), whereas in Matthew's it gives the form used habitually in the Synagogue, "*Our Father who art in heaven*". *Lk* gives one petition less than Matthew. In Matthew there is a phrase asking the liberation from evil, which is not present in Luke. But most of the prayer is the same in both versions.

Seeking God's kingdom and justice

The first part of the "Our Father" follows the precept "Seek first the kingdom of God and his justice" and the precept is directed in two ways. The first is in wanting the sanctification of the name of God, and his kingdom, a common element in Jewish prayers. To that Matthew adds the second understanding, of "wanting his will on earth as in heaven". This can be seen as the acceptance of everything which God causes to happen for us. Jesus himself gives an example of this in his prayer in the garden on the eve of his suffering and death. (*Mt* 26:39, *Mk* 14:36-37) We can also understand it as the voluntary commitment of all people who seek to accomplish the will of the Father in their lives.

Daily bread

We next look at what humans need, i.e., "daily bread" (*Mt* 6:11). The Greek *epiousios* ("daily") is a difficult word. Part of the problem of translating it is that it occurs only once in the entire New Testament. It may mean "general" or "normal". Without further use of the word its translation is uncertain.

The understanding of being fed by God "daily" in the history of the Christian church is diverse. Principally:

1. Material food.
   All people on earth need things to eat. We become part of that prayer when we help to provide for the needy. (We see this in Jesus' own life, e.g., in his compassion for the hungry and his miracles of feeding).

2. The Word of God.
   In the early Church being fed by God was often seen as being fed by his Word.

3. The Eucharist.
   The third sense, very much felt by some early Christians, was being fed daily by the Eucharist.

Forgiveness

The next petition concerns the pardoning of sins, or the cancelling of debt. The word "sin" and "debt" are identical in some Aramaic and Greek expressions.

There is a difference in the two versions: Matthew has "as we have forgiven", whereas Luke reads "for we forgive". In neither of them is it a reckoning. There is a sense of understanding that God is a "forgiver". We are to forgive as he forgives, not that the first forgiveness ever comes from man. We who recognise God's forgiveness, in recognising it fully, want to forgive others too.

Temptation

The final phrase asks God not to lead people into temptation. This does not imply that God normally tempts or tests people. ("Test" and "temptation" are the same word in Greek and Aramaic.) It may imply that God allows people to be tempted/tested. We remain confident because Jesus has prayed for us (see *Lk* 22) after himself having triumphed over Satan. The *"Deliver us from evil"* was later recognised as being part of the victory which Christ himself has won over the evil one. *"Deliver us from evil"* could equally be translated *"Deliver us from the evil one"*.

Concluding reflections

With the exception of the phrase "forgive us our trespasses", all the other petitions of the "Our Father" can be seen as Jesus' personal prayer, which he invites us to share. One of the key aspects of the new directions in Jesus' prayer is to teach us to ask for things from God whom we recognise as Father.

An image which appeals to me is of myself as a toddler, learning by asking my parents for one thing after another, understanding more as the responses are given, and growing in maturity through the interaction which takes place. The use of petition is part of the process of a child growing in understanding, in maturity, in trust and in awareness of the parents' love and guidance.

This image helps to overcome the Jewish hesitation about asking God for things, which may be due to the predominant image of God as all-powerful, unchangeable, and totally just. It is easier to ask when we see God as Father, in a family relationship. It is more difficult to have a good perspective on "asking for things" when the first vision of God is simply of power.

Parables about Prayer

In this chapter we look only at the parables of prayer recognised as key texts (*CCC* 2163), found in Luke's Gospel.

The importunate (bold) friend (*Lk* 11:5-13)

The first parable follows on from Jesus teaching the Our Father (*Lk* 11). It describes a midnight visit from a friend, asking for bread. *"I tell you though he will not get up and give it him because he is his friend, yet because of the man's boldness, he will get up and give him as much as he needs. So I say to you ask and it will be given to you, seek and you will find, knock and the door shall be opened to you, for everyone who asks receives... Which of your fathers, if his son asks for a fish will give him a snake, or asks for egg will give him a scorpion? ... If you then, though evil know how to give good gifts to your children, how much more will your father in heaven give the Holy Spirit to those who ask him".*

It is a compact parable, but within it there is much of interest, including things we might not expect. This parable follows directly Luke's set of petitions in the "Our Father", and the parable itself is also clearly about petition. It teaches perseverance. The first part of the parable considers two equal friends, wheras the second part puts before us a father and his son.

We first learn that we need persistence. This is then applied to a son/father relationship with the words, "ask, seek, knock". Next we are given examples of things asked and given. It is helpful to see symbolism in these: fish (a Christ symbol), a snake (a symbol of Satan), an egg (a symbol of new life/hope), a scorpion (a symbol of pain/death). We conclude with the strange phrase, *"How much more will your Father in heaven give the Holy Spirit to those who ask him?"*

"Asking and receiving" is a frequent theme in the synoptic Gospels. We see people beg of Jesus, and he gives, for example lepers, Jairus, Canaanite woman, good thief. We see, too, those who ask in silence, e.g., the bearers of the paralytic, the woman with the haemorrhage. We hear specific requests like that of the blind man, *"Son of David, have pity on me"*. In each instance Jesus recognises the need and responds. This parable first gives us symbolic images of what is asked and given, and then teaches us to ask for the Holy Spirit. Both are intended to draw us more deeply into the mystery of asking in prayer.

The importunate widow (*Lk* 18:1-8)

The second Lucan parable is "The importunate widow."
Then Jesus told his disciples a parable to show them that

they should always pray and not give up ... In a certain town there was a judge, who neither feared God nor cared about men. There was a widow in that town who kept coming to him ... "Give me justice against my adversary" ... for some time he refused ... but finally he said to himself, "Even though I don't fear God or care about men, yet because this widow keeps bothering me I will see that she gets justice, so that she doesn't wear me out with her coming." And the Lord said, "... listen to what the unjust judge says ... and will not God bring about justice to his chosen ones who cry to him day and night ... However, when the son of man comes will he find faith on earth?"

Again we have a compact and pithy parable. It is unusual among the parables in that we are told what it is about before the parable starts, ... "to show them that they should always pray (*proseuchomai*) and not give up". The Judge, a man who should be just, thinks instead only of himself and not of justice. He is set against a widow, a woman who has no power, no influence. The contrast is shown starkly. The widow's begging/petitioning, is not seen in the light of friendship as in the first parable, but simply in terms of badgering or bothering, or nagging. *"Will not God bring about justice for his chosen ones who cry out to him day and night, will he keep putting them off? I tell you he will see that they get justice and quickly."* Again we have a closing tag; *"However, when the Son of man comes will he find faith on earth?"* The title *"Son of Man"* is not explained, but helps us to look at Christ, his purpose, his mission and who he is. It talks of his coming again, and of the place of faith. The widow in prayer believed in justice. Despite the human representative of justice lacking virtue, her determination in petition achieved it. Her witness is given is given to encourage us in both faith and prayer.

The pharisee and the tax collector (*Lk* 18: 9-14)

The third parable is that of the Pharisee and the Tax collector. Jesus tells it to some *"who were confident of their own righteousness and looked down on everyone else. Two men went up to the temple to pray, one a Pharisee and the other a tax collector. ... The Pharisee stood up and prayed about himself ... God I thank you that I am not like other men... or even like this tax collector. .... But the tax collector stood at a distance and would not even look up to heaven. He said, "God have mercy on me, a sinner". ... I tell you that this man, rather than the other went home justified by God, for everyone who exalts himself will be made lowly, but the man who humbles himself will be exalted".*

We have here a great parable which gives an insight into Jesus' attitude towards sinners. It draws our attention to, and reminds us of, Jesus' own forgiveness of humble sinners in his broader ministry, e.g., His words to a paralysed man, *"Child, your sins are forgiven".* (*Mk* 2:5-10)

Jesus would later proclaim to the humble good thief, on the cross next to him, the promise of paradise. Perhaps this is the witness in Christ's life that most clearly matches the parable of the tax collector. The thief was the only person to whom Christ ever said, *"This day you will be with me in paradise"*. It wasn't any of his friends, not even his mother, but this fellow, rightly accused of doing wrong, who knew he deserved punishment, but who was contrite and humble. It is not necessary either to be well-practised in prayer, or to be a person of outstanding virtue, to receive forgiveness and blessings. A contrite heart is required.

Concluding reflections

Luke's parables about prayer start with an example of asking among equals (friends) and use symbols of fish, snakes, eggs and scorpions to indicate that the Father wants to give us what is good, not evil. The ideal gift is the Holy Spirit. The second parable shows someone weak, but determined, asking for justice from someone with power, who seems slow to use it for good. It commends persistence, concluding with a reminder of the need for faith. The third exalts the humble repentant sinner, showing how his contrite prayer is the fullness of what is needed, and how it is answered with love and forgiveness.

Jesus' Prayer in the Jewish Tradition

We take it for granted that Jesus was a person of prayer. We recognise that he was both a Jew who kept the tradition while also adding something new. This double image of Jewish tradition and personal innovation is a good place to start in our quest to understand his prayer.

Jesus the Jew

Jesus was fully Jewish; he was not only born of woman (a member of the human race) but he was also born *"Under the Law"* (i.e. fully a Jew) as St Paul says. (*Ga* 4:4) It is not easy for us as Christians to realise what this means. It indicates that Jesus' life was shaped by the Deuteronomic Code, (the law of Israel drawn from the first five books of the Bible), by traditions of the Jewish people, by their feasts and cultures. Jewish practice would have been at the heart of family life, of community life ... synagogue and temple.

The finding in the temple (*Lk 2*)

This is the first event in the synoptic Gospels which

points towards the Jewish tradition of prayer. Jesus at twelve years old went up to the temple with Mary and Joseph, taking part in the pilgrimage of Passover. When Mary and Joseph began the return journey, he stayed behind in Jerusalem. They went back to discover him among the teachers of the Law in the temple. On the one hand we see the normal tradition of a young Jew at that age taking on the responsibility to observe the Law personally and participate in prayer. On the other, we see Jesus' independence with respect to Mary and Joseph, following his own vocation. That vocation was religious, and to do with the house of God, *"Did you not know that I must be in the house of my Father."* This was something that Mary and Joseph did not then fully understand.

Zeal for his Father's house

Jesus' zeal for the cult of the temple was shown by his casting out of the money changers (*Mt* 21:12-17). He uses the quote from Isaiah referring to *the house of his Father ... which will be called the house of prayer for all nations* (*Is* 56:7). He cites Jeremiah too: *Has this house which is called in my name become a den of robbers?"* (*Jr* 7:7-11). The idea of an angry Jesus may seem odd to us, but it is clear that he has a great awareness of the sacredness of the temple. This seems to trigger in him the energy to cast out those who are defiling it.

Struggling against Satan

Jesus talks of prayer in the struggle against Satan ... *"there is a kind of demon that can only be driven out by prayer..."* (*Mk* 9:29). Earlier when he is tempted in the desert, (*Mt* 4:1-11) we find in Jesus' words a text from Deuteronomy. Deuteronomy 8:3 reads: *"And he humbled you and let you hunger and fed you with manna which you did not know, nor did your fathers know, that he might make you know that man does not live by bread alone but that man lives by everything that proceeds out of the mouth of the Lord."* Jesus quotes the second part of this verse almost verbatim and follows it with a quote from Psalm 90/91:10-12 concerning being supported by angels. In Jesus' struggle he brings to mind God's word in the Hebrew Scriptures. He uses Scripture in the battle against evil.

Starting ministry in the synagogue

Jewish community prayer, supported by the reading of Scriptures in synagogues, is a frequent starting point for Jesus' preaching ministry. Time and again he begins his preaching in the synagogue on the Sabbath, when Jews gather together for prayer and the word of God. (*Mt* 12:9-14, *Mk* 1:21-22, 3:1-6, 6:1 etc.)

Quoting Jewish Psalms, prayers and blessings

The Jewish prayer formulae were clearly part of Jesus' way of life, to the extent that when someone asked him what the greatest commandment was, out came the reply (*Mt* 22:37) based on the *"Shema"; "Hear, O Israel, the Lord your God is one Lord and you shall love the Lord your God with all your heart and with all your strength."* (*Dt* 6:4-7). This passage of Scripture is a regular daily prayer of the Jewish people.

The way in which Jesus teaches the keeping-holy of God's name in the Our Father is similar to the Jewish much-used prayer of eighteen benedictions, which bless God, his glory, his name, his strength, his power and his might. Similar words and phrases are found in Jesus' preaching on the Kingdom of God, the resurrection of the dead, and elsewhere.

When Pope Benedict, in "Jesus of Nazareth", reflects on the "Our Father" he sees its structure replicating that of the ten commandments, starting with the establishment of the primacy of God, leading naturally to a consideration of being human. Viewing the structure of the "Our Father" in this way also anchors Jesus' central prayer in the heart of the Jewish Tradition.

We rarely, if ever, see Jesus eating without first reciting a blessing, whether before sharing domestic meals, or before key events such as the multiplication of the loaves and the Last Supper. Such table blessings are standard Jewish tradition.

Not only do we see Jesus praying and quoting the psalms in all the Gospels. He also directs his followers to see himself as the fulfilment of the psalms: "*Everything written about me in the law of Moses and the prophets and the psalms must be fulfilled*" (Lk 24:44).

Concluding reflections

Jesus was imbued with the Jewish tradition of prayer and followed it habitually in daily life. He valued the sacredness of the temple and his ministry often flowed from the synagogue services. His meditation on and use of Scriptures in prayer is an example we can follow in our own prayer-life.

Jesus' Prayer beyond the Jewish Tradition

Theophanies, Father and Spirit

Two unique events concerning Jesus and his relationship in prayer with God the Father, are the theophanies, or the showings of the presence of God, which occur at the Baptism and the Transfiguration. In Mark's Gospel we hear the word of the Father to Jesus himself during the Baptism (*Mk* 1:11) and then to his disciples at the Transfiguration (in *Mk* 9:7). On both occasions Jesus is called the *"well-beloved son"*. We are also given the image of the Holy Spirit, described most fully in Luke's account, as *descending on him in bodily form, like a dove. (Lk 3: 21)*

Jesus is declared to be the Son of God. We also see the Spirit rest on him. This is important not only for Jesus' prayer but also for us. Both give a direction to his prayer distinct from that of traditional Judaism and give us a new aspect of our own relationship with God in prayer. Jesus addresses God as "Father" and teaches us to do the same. The Spirit comes down on Jesus at the two key occasions of the showing of God's presence. Our prayer, too, should involve sonship and the Spirit.

From the time of his baptism Jesus' prayer was a prayer of the Son to the Father. In the Hebrew Scriptures only 3% of the use of the word "father" refers to God. In the New Testament Scriptures the figure is 63%, many occasions of its use being in a context of prayer. Likewise, the place of The Spirit, too, becomes more clear and prominent in personal prayer.

Thanksgiving and rejoicing

There are two key occasions of thanksgiving in Jesus' prayer. The seventy sent out by Jesus return with joy saying *"Lord even the demons are subject to your name"*. (*Lk* 10:21), Jesus tells them, *"Nevertheless do not rejoice in this, that the Spirits are subject to you. Rejoice rather that your names are written in heaven"*.

We then read *"In that same hour he rejoiced in the Holy Spirit and said, 'I thank you Father, Lord of heaven and earth, that thou hast hidden these things from the wise and understanding and revealed them to babes....'"* (*Lk* 10:21-22). When Luke talks of Jesus *"rejoicing in the Holy Spirit"*, he uses the Greek word *"agalliasato"* , which expresses intense emotion of joy.

A further powerful expression of thanks is found at the raising of Lazarus. *"So they took away the stone and he lifted up his eyes and said, 'Father I thank thee that thou hast heard me. I knew that you have heard me, but I have said this on account of those that are standing by....'"* (*Jn* 11:41). Jesus, although he doesn't specifically instruct people to thank God in prayer, gives his own witness to it, which is powerful. The rejoicing which accompanies the thanksgiving is for us, too, a strong witness and an example to follow.

Praying alone

Elsewhere in the synoptic Gospels we glean further insights into Jesus' prayer. He seeks to spend time in prayer alone. Such praying alone is, for him, profound, even to the extent of his praying alone all night when there are important decisions to be made. We don't know if his prayer was silent or vocal, or how it was carried out. We do know that it was personal and in a separate place. He committed himself to it when there were other demands on his time. It was clearly important to him. His witness calls us to similar commitment.

Jesus, anguish, suffering, and glory

Later in Jesus' life we see him praying while suffering. (*Mt* 27:46, *Mk* 15: 34, *Lk* 23:46) John's Gospel is slightly different to the synoptics. John is distinct in portraying Jesus' suffering as a way to glory.

Jesus prays as he embarks on his "hour". Reading through chapters twelve to seventeen of John's Gospel we find his understanding of Jesus' glory in its full context. The account of Jesus' sacrifice gradually unfolds as he shows that he loves his own people to the very end. He shows how perfect his love is by washing the disciples' feet (*Jn* 13:1-13) and giving them the mandate "*Love one another as I have loved you*" (*Jn* 13:34).

Jesus was to pass from this world to the Father. The account continues as Jesus says, "*I am praying for them; I am not praying for the world but for those whom thou hast given me, for they are thine, and thine are mine, and I am glorified in them*" (*Jn* 17:9). We see a deeper, eternal bond, which has been formed between us and the Father through Jesus' life and generous sacrifice. Love leads to glory. It is on such an image of glory that the early Christian church, and indeed the whole Christian tradition has built its prayer and its hope.

In Mark's Gospel, in contrast, Jesus addresses the Father as "Abba" with a degree of familiarity ... "Daddy" (*Mk* 14:36), making a plea that if it be possible death should pass him by, but also showing total subservience to the Father's will.

The prayers on the cross too, vary in the different Gospel accounts. In Mark and Matthew's accounts we see the recitation of Psalm 21/22, " ... *My God, My God, why have you forsaken me?*" (*Mk* 15:34, *Mt* 27:46).

Earlier in Luke's Gospel we see Jesus' anguish concerning the coming misfortunes of the nation and the holy city, Jerusalem (*Lk* 21:24, 23:28). We see him interceding on behalf of his captors. As he is being crucified Jesus prays for those who are killing him, *"Father, forgive them; for they know not what they do"* (*Lk* 23:34) then at the point of death cries to his father, *"Father, into your hands I commend my spirit"*(*Lk* 23:46). In his prayers here he gives us the double witness through his own suffering:

  i. of petition for freedom from sin for others, and
  ii. of total self-giving to his Father. (He "commends his spirit" to the Father)

These are our models too.

Concluding reflections

Jesus' prayer went beyond the Jewish tradition. This is shown especially in the theophanies, in his thanksgiving and rejoicing, and in his suffering and glory. The Spirit, too, comes upon Jesus at the theophanies. (The connection with the Spirit is made clearer in the next chapter on Paul). Jesus' sacrifice, his glory, his petition to the Father and his total self-giving are all recounted powerfully. These help us in our own prayer, and give us ever-deeper hope.

Paul and Prayer

Paul's teaching on prayer is rich, but not always straightforward. This chapter includes a number of diverse texts to help us to understand Paul's practice and his teaching on prayer.

Influential texts in the early Church

Two texts of Paul deserve a mention because of the debate they gave rise to in the early Christian Church.

1. The first text is 1 Thessalonians 5:17. Paul says "Pray without ceasing" using the Greek word *proseuchomai*, which means "ask" or "request". Early church writers wondered, "How can you pray at all times e.g. when you sleep, when your mind is doing administrative tasks etc.?"

2. The second text, which helped to widen the definition of the word "pray", is the list in 1 Timothy 2:1. Paul gives a collection of words, "entreaties, prayers, pleas, and thanksgivings". He goes on to explain that these should be offered for those in authority. Some early Christian writers, however, thought the list might constitute a system, a structure, or a group of activities which

ought to go together. So the meaning of prayer was stretched by some writers in the second and third centuries so that it could be seen as an activity including all these different elements.

Paul's background and experiences

Some aspects of Paul's background and of his understanding of prayer make him stand out from the evangelists, the Old Testament writers, and the other New Testament letter writers. Before his conversion Paul had rabbinic training (under Gamaliel). He had a rich background in the Jewish Tradition. Much of Paul's understanding of prayer comes from his Jewish roots. That almost goes without saying. But added to this are further personal characteristics.

Christ in Paul

Paul has a strong understanding of his personal sharing in the suffering of the death of Christ (e.g., in 2 *Co* 4:10) and he shows powerful emotional ties which attach him to Christ. Paul saw that Christ *loved him and gave himself up for him* (*Ga* 2:20), and Christ, having done this, had somehow entered into Paul's life, so that Paul describes his life in these terms: "*It is not I that live, but rather Christ that lives in me.*" (*Ga* 2:20) This awareness of Christ in his personal life is very powerful. St

Augustine of Hippo would later describe God's presence in his life as, *"more inward than my most inward part and higher than the highest element within me"*. The awareness of the "divine presence living inside us" seems to me a tremendous gift and a powerful, almost visceral, impetus to prayer. We should ask God for this gift and treasure it.

The Spirit

In the letter to the Romans we read: *"For all who are led by the Spirit of God are sons of God, for you did not receive the spirit of slavery in order to fall back into fear, but you have received the spirit of sonship. When you cry, "Abba, Father", it is the Spirit himself, bearing witness with our spirit, that we are the children of God."* (8:14-16)

We see Paul's association of the "Spirit" with the "spiritual sonship" which we share. The awareness of the Spirit in our prayer life, is even more profound towards the end of the same chapter: *"Likewise the Spirit helps us in our weakness, for we do not know how to pray, but the Spirit himself intercedes for us with sighs too deep for words, and God who searches the heart of men knows what is the mind of the Spirit, because the Spirit intercedes for the saints according to the will of God"* (8:26-27)

The Spirit is seen by Paul as a great influence on behaviour in the Christian assembly. Paul, in addition to associating the Spirit with spiritual sonship, also associates the Spirit with the community and with order in the community. The Spirit builds up the Church, even when glossolalia, i.e., praying aloud in tongues (1 *Co* 14:2) and spontaneous enthusiasms (1 *Co* 12:3), are present. Paul gives a caution concerning the need for discernment in what is said or shared, and he counsels that what is done should be for the common good. Leaders need to be discerning, and the meeting should be without scandal: *"For God is not a God of confusion, but of peace"* (1 *Co* 14:33). So, on the one hand, we have a sense of the Spirit bubbling out, pouring out his gifts on God's children. On the other we see that the body of Christ needs to function in an orderly, peaceful way. The members of the Church are Christ's body: unity and concord between the different parts are needed for the body to function well.

When Paul talks of the Spirit in prayer he has two perspectives. Firstly the Spirit is a fountain of the energy of God's joy. This wells up in the individual, guiding, forming and encouraging him/her in prayer. Secondly the same Spirit is also working in the community, maintaining it in peace and harmony, but with each community member having their own calling, building up the body of Christ.

Paul's prayer habits

Thanksgiving and petition

The triple dynamic of, i. the presence of the Spirit, ii. the sense of Christ in us, and iii. thanksgiving, impels Paul to petition, again and again. Paul asks ... he asks frequently for grace, he asks for the true life of faith, he asks for the good news to be shared, he asks for steadfastness in faith when the Church begins to feel persecution. He asks not only for those to whom he ministers, but he asks that they themselves regularly pray for their leaders, their shepherds. This ties in with the sense of a need for order, and the need for prayer to maintain the church in harmony.

In the letter to Philemon, he goes from thanks to petition in typical manner: *"I thank my God always when I remember you in my prayers because I hear of your love and your faith which you have towards the Lord Jesus and the saints and I pray that the sharing of your faith may promote the knowledge and all that is good in Christ."* He expects that those things for which he thanks God will continue to be fruitful and will build up God's kingdom.

Paul frequently asked others to pray for him and for his companions ... *Pray for us, brethren, as I do for you.*

Paul's frequent requests for prayer are a good example for us to do the same.

Expectation

Paul expects Christ to come again soon. His cry is *"Maranatha"*, Aramaic for "Come Lord", (1 *Co.* 16:22). There is an urgency ... prayers are expected to be answered quickly so that the kingdom of God will be built in time for the Lord to come again.

Concluding reflections

Prayer is personal and communal, urgent and emotional. It is filled with Christ and filled with the Spirit. It derives from joy in the victory of Christ, won by his suffering, death and resurrection. So Paul's prayer seems completely different and fresh. It also has the same heart as Christ's own prayer. Paul's perspective of the wider body of Christ includes a profusion of gifts and service, but in harmony and unity.

The "body" is an important concept for Paul. The Church itself is the body of Christ. Christ and the Spirit also fill the "body" of the person who prays. I receive Christ into my own body in the Eucharist. I find that Paul's words *"no longer I that live ... Christ lives in me"*, affirms that truth of Christ's presence in my life and encourages me to ask him to enter-in more deeply.

The Letter to the Hebrews

Perhaps when you were reading Chapter Four (Sacrifice), you wondered, "Was God leading his people down the wrong track? If God wanted them to communicate well with him, why didn't he start by teaching them to ask, to praise, to say 'thank you', 'sorry' and the like?" Chronologically God seems to have put priesthood and sacrifice before those actions which we more commonly think of as "prayer".

But the question, "Why put sacrifice first, why imprint sacrifice on human minds before all other aspects of the Covenant?" does not, and should not go away. Full freedom from sin, death and every evil comes ultimately not through petitionary prayer, but through one perfect sacrifice. To see "petitionary prayer" as greater than "sacrifice" is impossible when we grasp the mystery of Easter, the fullness of Christ's mission, his deepest gift to us.

The letter to the Hebrews is a key text of the New Testament because it names Jesus as "priest". It talks of Christ's priesthood and draws us into a deeper understanding. It leads us again to the mystery of prayer, sacrifice and union with God. The truth is revealed. The sacrifice of Jesus is not only the most perfect sacrifice possible, but also the most powerful intercession of all time. The full power and depth of it cannot be surpassed.

Hebrews tells us that Christ, on our behalf, entered not the sanctuary of the temple, but heaven itself. (*Heb* 9:24) By Christ's "*single offering he has perfected for all time those who are sanctified*". (*Heb* 10:14) Nowhere in Scripture is the word "prayer" associated with that which is "perfect", but here Christ's sacrifice is "perfect". It achieves the fullness of freedom from evil.

The mystery of the power of prayer associated with Jesus' sacrifice encourages us to have "*confidence to enter the sanctuary by the blood of Jesus, by the new and living way which he opened for us through the curtain, that is through his flesh.*" (*Heb* 10:19)

To me the letter to the Hebrews is a reminder of the central event of Jesus' own sacrifice for us. That sacrifice opens a new way for us to come before God's throne.

I am a Catholic priest. The true sacrificial nature of the Mass, the celebration of the Eucharist, which makes present in sacramental form the same sacrifice of Christ, is at the daily heart of my spiritual life. Prayers of intercession, which I make at all times of day, in all places and circumstances, receive their deepest power through the same sacrifice of Christ. My own varied prayers of thanks find their power and relevance through my gratitude for Christ's suffering, dying and rising. The efficacy and the power of Christ's sacrifice are pre-eminent. His sacrifice frees me from sin, death and every evil. In prayers and devotions associated with the Eucharist, the awareness of Christ's generous sacrifice and love is central. For me the letter to the Hebrews reminds me of two important truths about prayer:

1. In view of the priestly sacrifice of Jesus and its power, all prayer of mine now seeks to be in union with that one perfect sacrifice. For me this particularly concerns prayers of intercession, petition and thanksgiving.

2. The Eucharistic celebration makes present sacramentally that same living sacrifice. In union with the fullness of the mystery of Christ's sacrifice, my prayer finds its deepest meaning and purpose.

Concluding reflections

The letter to the Hebrews presents Jesus as the priest whose sacrifice is perfect. Its power to free humankind from evil far surpasses any prayer of petition. This helps me to see my prayer in union with Christ. The power of prayer is not independent of Christ's perfect sacrifice, but finds its deepest purpose and power in that sacrifice.

Conclusion

I ask the reader to ponder the Scriptures further, with the question "What can they teach us about prayer?" The texts on which I have reflected here are only a small selection of the prayer-texts in the Bible. I hope that in presenting them I have not simplified anything to the point where this brings inaccuracy. God gives us, through the Scriptures, a rich variety of images. Depending on which we use, our perception of prayer changes. As one image follows another so our awareness of prayer deepens. This book does not teach the whole journey, merely a few insights or stepping-stones, which I have found to be helpful and inspiring. I hope that they may also have helped you.

Further Reading

Catechism of the Catholic Church [CCC] (Burns & Oates, London 1999) covers the theology and catechesis of early biblical prayer and creation in *CCC* 2556-2569. For the understanding of the prayer of contemplation and its definitions see 2709-2724.

The Anchor Bible Dictionary. Freedman (ed.) Doubleday New York 1992. (various articles)

Useful reflections on prayer and creation, Trinity, community, Original sin etc., can be found in "*The World of Prayer*" by Adrienne Von Speyr. Ignatius Press, San Francisco, 1985 (a translation of "*Die Welt des Gebetes*" published in German in 1951). This is a major source of material in Chapters one and two.

The mystery of the prayer of contemplation is covered in great detail in the *Dictionnaire de Spiritualité* [DS] (Beauchesne, Paris, 1935-1992) tome 2 pp1643-2193. I also rely heavily on the article "*Prière*" in the DS tome 12 pp 2196-2347, both for specific and general insights into New Testament prayer.

Good general backgrounds to prayer are found in "*Prayer – A Study in the History and Psychology of Religion*" by Friedrich Heiler (OUP 1932).

A good range of example prayers is found in "*The Prayers of Man*" by Alfonso M di Nola. Heinmann, London 1962.

General scriptural understanding of New Testament prayer can be found in, Cullman, O, *"Prayer in the New Testament"* SCM Press London 1995

A good introduction to the topic of the beatific vision is found in Cardinal Pierre Paul Philippe's *"La Vita di Preghiera"*, Libreria Editrice Vaticana 1997 pp 21-41

For good studies of Hebrew scriptural prayer I suggest: Greenberg, M, *"Biblical Prose Prayer"* University of California Press, Berkley. 1983

To understand Jewish prayer I commend the introduction to: Singer, Rev S (Jakobovits I ed.) *"The Authorised Daily Prayer book of the United Hebrew Congregations of the Commonwealth"*, Singer's Prayer Book Committee, 1990.

For more details on Jesus' prayer see: Marshall, H, *"Jesus, Example and Teacher of Prayer in the New Testament"*, in *"Into God's Presence"* ed. Longenecker, RN, Eerdmans, Cambridge, U.K. 2001, especially pp 127-128.

Scripture Quotations

The Psalms Grail Version, CTS London 2003

Other Scriptures *The Holy Bible RSV* (Catholic Edn.) CTS London 1966.

Teachings on Prayer

From very early on many methods and styles and definitions of prayer have flowered within the Church. This booklet explores the writings and books of the most important Fathers of the Church and Saints and maps the spiritual history and inter-relations between the different styles of prayer.

The Deeper Christianity Series delves into the mysteries of Christianity, opening up the spiritual treasures of the Church.

Fr Taylerson is a parish priest in rural East Staffordshire. He is a former Spiritual Director and a current external tutor at Oscott College.

ISBN: 978 1 86082 483 8

CTS Code: SP 22

A world of Catholic reading
at your fingertips ...

CTS

... now online
Browse 500 titles at

www.cts-online.org.uk

Catholic Faith, Life, and Truth for all

Deepening Prayer

Prayer is at the heart of the Christian life, but is always a battle. This booklet explores some of the major methods of Christian prayer, as well as the problems and pitfalls. Sr Mary David uses the wisdom of the Church Fathers to lead people of today into a deeper relationship with God.

The Deeper Christianity Series delves into the mysteries of Christianity, opening up the spiritual treasures of the Church.

Sr Mary David is a nun of the Benedictine community of St Cecilia's Abbey in Ryde on the Isle of Wight.

ISBN: ISBN 978 1 86082 382 4

CTS Code: SP 13